A Child's History of Britain

Life in the Stone Age, Bronze Age and Iron Age

Anita Ganeri

Raintree is an imprint of Capstone Global Library
Limited, a company incorporated in England and Wales
having its registered office at 7 Pilgrim Street, London,
EC4V 6LB – Registered company number: 6695582

www.raintreepublishers.co.uk
myorders@raintreepublishers.co.uk

Edited by Clare Lewis and Holly Beaumont
Designed by Richard Parker
Original illustration © Capstone Global Library Ltd 2014
Illustrated by: Norbert Sipos (pp.26-7), Beehive
Illustration
Picture research by Pam Mitsakos
Originated by Capstone Global Library Ltd
Production by Helen McCreath
Printed and bound in China

ISBN 978 1 406 28562 8
18 17 16 15 14
10 9 8 7 6 5 4 3 2

British Library Cataloguing in Publication Data
A full catalogue record for this book is available from the
British Library.

Acknowledgements

We would like to thank the following for permission
to reproduce photographs: Alamy pp. 12 (© Sabena
Jane Blackbird), 27 top (© John Warburton-Lee
Photography), 27 bottom (© Powered by Light/Alan
Spencer); Art Resource, NY pp. 10 (© The Trustees
of the British Museum), 20 (Werner Forman); The
Bridgeman Art Library pp. 7 (Musee des Antiquites
Nationales, St. Germain-en-Laye, France / Giraudon),
16 (Royal Albert Memorial Museum, Exeter, Devon,
UK), 18 (LatitudeStock); Corbis p. 11 (© Skyscan); Dover
Museum p. 13 (Dover Museum and Bronze Age Boat
Gallery); Dreamstime p. 19 (Thomas Langlands); Mary
Evans pp. 6 (Natural History Museum), 22 (Mary Evans
Picture Library/Town & Country Planning); Newscom
p. 15 (whphotos114230); Science Source p. 21 (Carlos
Muñoz-Yagüe); Shutterstock pp. 5 (Fulcanelli), 9
(Antonin Vinter), 23 (Jason Benz Bennee), 25 (Adrian
Reynolds); Superstock p. 8 (imagebroker.net); Wikimedia
pp. 14 (Ian and Viv Hamilton), 17 (Jim Champion), 24
(Midnightblueowl).

Cover image of family life in the Iron Age reproduced
with permission of the Bridgeman Art Library (© English
Heritage Photo Library).

We would like to thank Dr Oliver J.T. Harris of the
University of Leicester for his invaluable help in the
preparation of this book.

Every effort has been made to contact copyright holders
of material reproduced in this book. Any omissions will
be rectified in subsequent printings if notice is given to
the publishers.

Contents

Some words are shown in bold, **like this**. You can find out what they mean by looking in the glossary.

Stone, bronze and iron

People have lived in Britain for hundreds of thousands of years. In 2010, **archaeologists** found around 80 stone tools near the village of Happisburgh (pronounced "haze-bruh") in Norfolk. The tools are thought to be at least 800,000 years old, making them the oldest signs of our **ancestors** in Britain.

The time between the first humans and the arrival of the Romans in Britain is known as **prehistoric** Britain. It is divided into different ages, called the Stone Age, Bronze Age and Iron Age. They were named because people first made their tools from stone, then later from the metals bronze and iron.

PREHISTORIC BRITAIN

About 800,000 years ago – 2500 BC	**Stone Age**
about 800,000–10,000 years ago	Palaeolithic (Old Stone Age)
about 10,000–6,000 years ago	Mesolithic (Middle Stone Age)
about 6,000–4,500 years ago	Neolithic (New Stone Age)
About 2500–800 BC	**Bronze Age**
About 800 BC–AD 43	**Iron Age**

Stonehenge in Wiltshire is the most famous prehistoric monument in Britain.

CLUES TO THE PAST

Apart from stone tools, archaeologists have found many other objects from prehistoric Britain. They include weapons, jewellery, boats, **tombs** and even long-dead bodies. From these, archaeologists have been able to piece together a fascinating picture of how people lived such a long time ago.

Who lived in the Stone Age?

The people who lived in Britain at the start of the Stone Age probably walked across what is now the English Channel and North Sea. At that time, Britain was not an island but part of mainland Europe. Over the next hundreds of thousands of years, the **climate** changed many times. For long periods, Britain was covered in ice and people were driven away by the cold.

Boxgrove Man

In the 1990s, **archaeologists** found an ancient leg bone in a gravel pit in the village of Boxgrove in West Sussex. It belonged to a Stone Age man who lived at least 500,000 years ago. So far, this is the earliest human bone found in Britain.

This is what Boxgrove Man may have looked like. He was fit and strong, and around 1.8 metres (6 feet) tall.

HANDY AXES

The Stone Age gets its name because people made their tools from a type of stone called **flint**. Hitting the flint into shape was called flint knapping. Some of the earliest flint tools were hand axes. These had sharp edges for cutting, and a round base for fitting into your hand. You used hand axes for cutting meat, scraping animal skins and digging up roots.

How would I find food?

If you lived in the early Stone Age, you collected nuts, roots and berries for food. You also went fishing and hunted wild animals, such as mammoths and deer. You ate their meat and used their skin for making clothes. Hunters only had simple wooden spears, so catching animals could be difficult. Sometimes they chased the animals into bogs or off cliffs to make this easier.

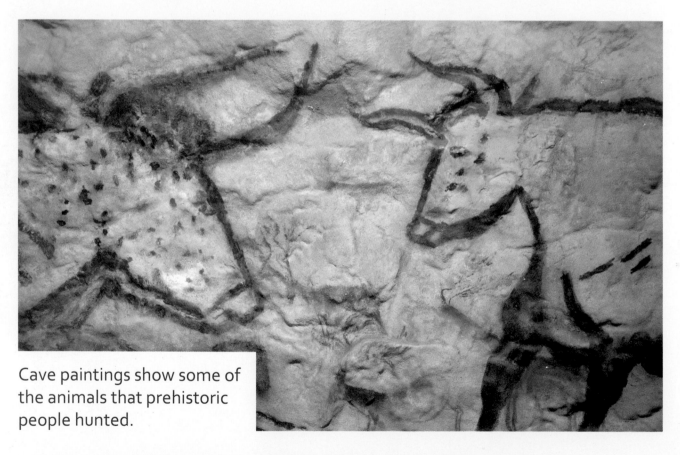

Cave paintings show some of the animals that prehistoric people hunted.

Later in the Stone Age, people began to build houses and settle in one place, instead of following the animals they hunted. They grew crops and kept animals. The first farms in Britain appeared in around 4000 **BC**.

SKARA BRAE

The ruins of the Stone Age village of Skara Brae lie in the Orkney Islands, in Scotland. People lived there from about 3100–2500 BC. The village had eight stone houses and a workshop, with roofs made from thick moss. The houses were partly built below the ground to keep them out of the wind.

What would I believe?

Early in the Stone Age, the animals you hunted played a large part in your beliefs. In some places, people collected the skulls of the animals that they had killed. Hunters may have worn these as headdresses, to disguise themselves while they were hunting, or as part of special ceremonies to bring good luck in the hunt.

This stag's skull from Star Carr in Yorkshire dates from around 7500 BC. It has two holes cut into it so that a person could tie it to their head using leather straps.

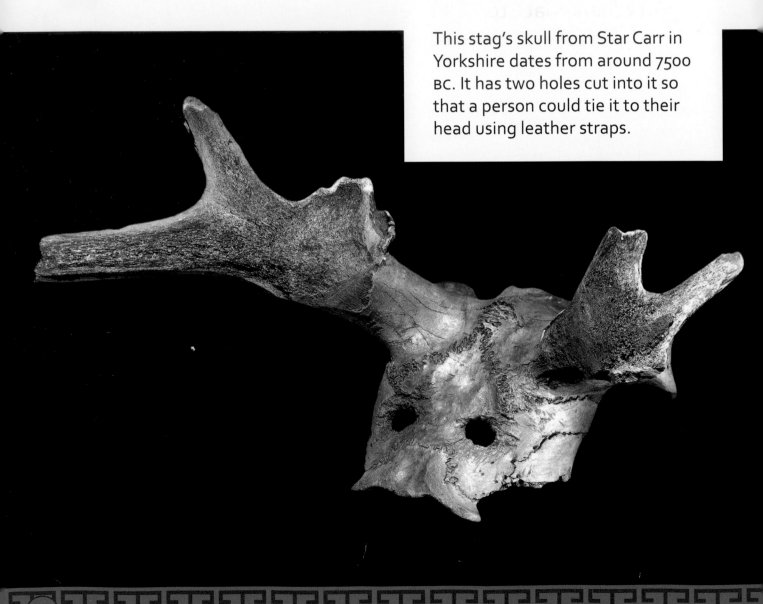

Later on, people began to take great care in how they buried their dead. They built huge monuments, called **barrows**, to mark their graves. West Kennet Long Barrow in Wiltshire was built in around 3600 **BC**. It is a long mound of earth with several stone burial **chambers** built inside. **Archaeologists** have found the remains of around 50 people inside, including both adults and children.

Experts think that Stonehenge was also a burial ground or a centre of religious ceremonies.

SUNLIT TOMB

One of the most amazing Stone Age **tombs** was built at Newgrange in Ireland in around 3200 BC. It has four burial chambers, covered by an enormous mound of stones and turf. The tomb was carefully designed so that, on the shortest day of the year (in the middle of winter), the sun shone through a hole above the door straight into the main burial chamber.

West Kennet Long Barrow is over 90 metres (295 feet) long.

How was metal important in the Bronze Age?

If you lived in Britain in around 2500 **BC**, a new discovery was about to change your life. For the first time, people started making tools, weapons, jewellery and other objects from metal, instead of stone. At first, people used copper but later they discovered how to make bronze. This is a mixture of copper and tin, which is harder and stronger than either of those materials.

These bronze axe heads were discovered in a field in Lincolnshire.

The remains of the Dover boat on display at Dover Museum. Originally, it would have measured more than 18 metres (59 feet) in length.

TRADING BOAT

In 1992, **archaeologists** found the remains of a wooden trading boat buried under a road near Dover in Kent. It was built in around 1500 BC to carry people and goods, such as metal tools and weapons, across the English Channel.

Huge copper mines were dug in Wales and Ireland during the Bronze Age. The enormous Great Orme copper mine in Wales may have been the largest in the world. Men, women and children all worked in the mines, crawling along dark, cramped tunnels to reach the precious metals.

Where would I live and what would I wear?

If you lived in the Stone Age, your home was probably rectangular, with a thatched roof. If you lived in the Bronze Age, your home was a roundhouse with a cone-shaped roof. You had a fire in the centre of your house for warmth, light and cooking.

Your house may have been part of a group to protect it from raiders.

Clothes and jewellery

By the late Bronze Age, people were weaving woollen cloth for making into clothes. Women wore short woollen **tunics** and long skirts. Men wore knee-length woollen skirts with tunics, cloaks and round woollen hats. They were **clean-shaven** and had long hair. Children probably wore smaller versions of their parents' clothes.

Bronze Age metalsmiths made beautiful jewellery from bronze and gold. Many rings, brooches and bracelets have been found, buried in the ground. Some were probably left by their owners who planned to collect them later on. Others were religious offerings.

The Mold gold cape was probably worn by a woman or child because it is so small.

CAPE OF GOLD

A beautiful **cape** of beaten gold was found in a Bronze Age grave near Mold in Wales. It is more than 3,600 years old. The cape was badly crushed, but it was pieced back together again.

What would I believe?

It seems that Bronze Age people believed in life after death. They buried their dead in graves, covered by small, round **barrows**. They also buried objects, such as pottery, daggers and jewellery, for the dead to use in the afterlife.

Bronze Age people also placed precious objects, such as swords, in rivers and marshes. These are thought to have been offerings to the gods to ask for a favour, such as a good harvest.

Found at a Bronze Age barrow in Farway in Devon, these objects include a stone cup.

Barrows became important gathering places. They were carefully placed in the landscape so that they could be seen from far away.

Bronze Age burials

Bush Barrow is one of several Bronze Age barrows found close to Stonehenge. It is one of the richest graves found in Britain. A man was buried inside, lying on his side, surrounded by precious goods, including an axe and two large daggers. From the high quality of these objects, experts think the man must have been very important.

ARCHER'S GRAVE

The grave of a Bronze Age **archer** was discovered in 2002 close to Stonehenge. It dates to around 2300 **BC**. Buried with the man were about 100 objects, including copper knives, pots and **flint** arrowheads.

Where would I live in the Iron Age?

If you were a child in the Iron Age, you would probably have lived in a roundhouse, similar to a Bronze Age home. Your house was built of wood, covered with clay and animal dung, with a thatched, cone-shaped roof.

Hill forts were built on hilltops because they were easier to defend. They were surrounded by ditches and banks of earth to keep attackers out. Some hill forts had villages inside and formed important trade centres. Others were used as hiding places in wartime.

Maiden Castle in Dorset is one of the biggest Iron Age hill forts in Europe.

If you lived in Scotland or Ireland, your home might have been a **crannog**. A crannog was a human-made island, built of stone and wood on a lake or the edge of a marsh. One or two roundhouses were built on top, with a wooden fence around them. Because they could only be reached by boat or across a narrow causeway, crannogs were difficult to attack.

Archaeologists have rebuilt this crannog at Loch Tay in Scotland.

CELTIC TRIBES

The people of the Iron Age are sometimes called Celts. They spoke similar languages and lived in a similar way, but they were not one group of people. There were many different groups, or tribes, of Celts, each with its own ruler, or chief.

What would I believe?

Iron Age people worshipped many gods and goddesses. They believed that these gods had power over nature and controlled what happened in people's lives. People made offerings of precious metalwork, such as jewellery and weapons, to the gods. They also made **sacrifices** of animals and humans.

Found in the River Thames, this shield was probably an offering to the gods.

Bog bodies

Some Iron Age bodies have been dug up from bogs around Britain. One of the most famous bodies was found at Lindow Moss, Cheshire, and is known as Lindow Man. The man was about 25 years old when he died around 2,000 years ago. It seems that he was violently killed, then his body was dropped into the bog. Experts think that he may have been chosen to be sacrificed to the gods.

This is what Lindow Man might have looked like.

DRUIDS

Iron Age priests were called druids. We do not know very much about them, but experts think that they carried out religious ceremonies and knew how to make medicines from plants and herbs. It is thought that they trained for several years and passed on their secret knowledge by word of mouth.

What would I do when I grew up?

In the Iron Age, your family were probably farmers. They grew crops, such as wheat, barley and beans, and kept animals, such as cows, pigs and sheep. Some grain was ground into flour for making bread. Some was stored in grain pits for use in winter. You helped your parents in the fields and at home, making food and doing chores.

War and warriors

Most Iron Age people were also warriors. You might fight when defending your own village or if you were raiding another tribe's village to steal their cattle. In battle, you were armed with a sword, shield and spear, and sometimes painted your body with blue dye to make yourself look more frightening.

An artist's idea of what life might have looked like in the Iron Age.

METALWORK

During the Iron Age, people started to use iron for making tools and weapons. Ironworking became a very important job. Metalsmiths also made beautiful jewellery, such as torcs. These were thick neck rings, made from twisted strands of silver and gold wire.

This beautiful torc is made from 64 strands of gold and silver.

The end of the Iron Age

The ruins of a Roman fort at Richborough in Kent.

By the 1st century **BC,** the Romans had conquered large parts of Europe and now turned their attention to Britain. The Roman general Julius Caesar invaded Britain in 55 and 54 BC, but returned to Rome each time.

Nearly a hundred years later, in **AD** 43, the Roman **emperor** Claudius sent another army to conquer Britain. With 40,000 men, Claudius conquered the southern half of Britain, and set up a new capital at Camulodunum (Colchester in Essex). Then Claudius returned home, and his generals prepared to move further north and west.

Some Iron Age tribes agreed to obey Roman laws and pay taxes, in return for keeping their lands. Others tried to fight back but within a few years the Romans ruled large parts of Britain and the Roman way of life had taken over.

REVOLT!

In AD 61, the Iceni tribe from East Anglia launched a daring rebellion against the Romans. Led by their queen, Boudicca, the Iceni marched to Camulodunum and attacked the town. Next, they attacked and burned London, leaving hundreds of people dead. Eventually, the Iceni were defeated by the Romans and, it is thought, Boudicca poisoned herself.

This bronze statue of Boudicca stands in central London.

How do we know?

Built in around 600 **BC**, Castell Henllys is an Iron Age hill fort in Pembrokeshire, Wales. **Archaeologists** have been digging at the site for more than 20 years. Using archaeological evidence from the site, they have rebuilt four roundhouses and a grain store. Inside, they have furnished the houses as they would have been in the Iron Age, with beds, weaving **looms** and cooking fires. Visitors can learn how people lived and even try their hand at grinding flour and making Iron Age bread.

In the middle of the roundhouse was a fire for cooking and heating.

Wool was woven into clothes and blankets on looms like this.

Map

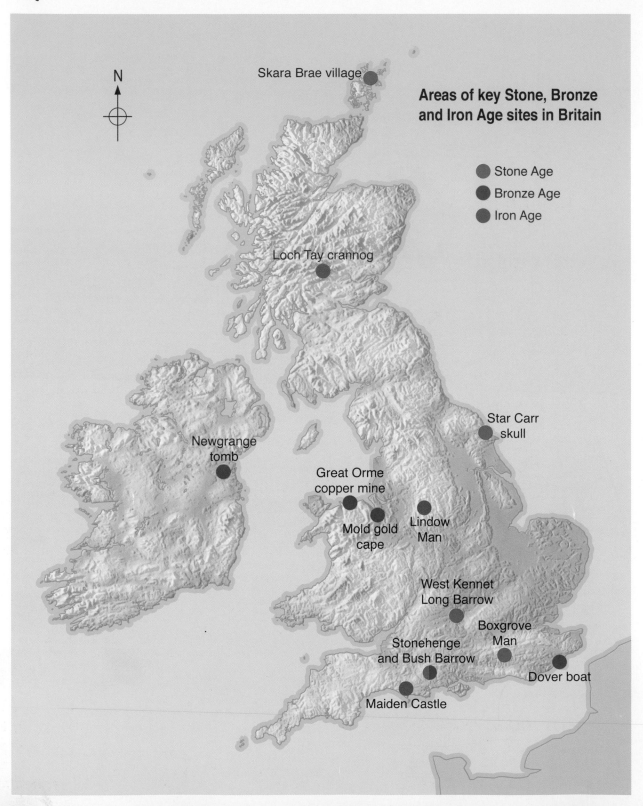

Skara Brae village

Areas of key Stone, Bronze and Iron Age sites in Britain

- Stone Age
- Bronze Age
- Iron Age

Loch Tay crannog

Star Carr skull

Newgrange tomb

Great Orme copper mine

Mold gold cape

Lindow Man

West Kennet Long Barrow

Boxgrove Man

Stonehenge and Bush Barrow

Dover boat

Maiden Castle

Quiz

What do you know about life in the Stone, Bronze and Iron ages? Try this quiz to find out!

1. What was flint used for?
   a making bread
   b making jewellery
   c making tools

2. What did Bronze Age people make clothes from?
   a wool
   b animal fur
   c silk

3. Where were Bronze Age people buried?
   a in rivers
   b in barrows
   c in forests

4. What was a crannog?
   a Iron Age drink
   b Iron Age sword
   c Iron Age home

5. How would you wear a torc?
   a around your neck
   b around your wrist
   c around your waist

Glossary

AD dates after the birth of Christ; these count upwards, so AD 20 is earlier than AD 25

ancestor person who lived before us, a very long time ago

archaeologist person who finds and studies places and objects from the past

archer soldier who fights with a bow and arrows

barrow earth mound, built to mark where people were buried

BC dates before the birth of Christ; these count downwards, so 25 BC is earlier than 20 BC

cape cloak-like piece of clothing or jewellery

chamber room-like space

clean-shaven man who does not have a beard or moustache

climate weather in a place over a long period of time

crannog Iron Age home built on stilts above a lake

emperor person who rules an empire (a group of states and territories under the rule of one country)

flint stone used for making tools and weapons

loom machine used for turning wool into cloth

prehistoric from a time before things were written down

sacrifice something given to please a god or goddess

tomb place where a dead person is buried

tunic long, sleeveless, dress-like shirt

Find out more

Books

Cut-throat Celts, Terry Deary (Scholastic, 2008)

Prehistoric Britain, Alex Frith (Usborne, 2010)

Savage Stone Age, Terry Deary (Scholastic, 2008)

Stone Age to Iron Age (Early British History), Claire Throp (Raintree, 2014)

Websites

www.bbc.co.uk/history/handsonhistory/ancient-britain.shtml
Make a stone circle and create some cave art with this BBC website.

www.pastexplorers.org.uk/fun/prehistory
www.pastexplorers.org.uk/fun/ironage
These two web pages come from the Past Explorers website about the Stone, Bronze and Iron ages, and the amazing objects found by archaeologists.

www.show.me.uk/topicpage/Prehistory.html
Have a look at this website for information and fun activities, based around various prehistoric sites in Britain.

Places to visit

There are lots of Stone, Bronze and Iron Age sites to visit in many parts of Britain. You can find out more through the following organisations:

English Heritage
www.english-heritage.org.uk

The National Trust in England, Wales and Northern Ireland
www.nationaltrust.org.uk

The National Trust of Scotland
www.nts.org.uk

Index